The Grumpy Old Man's Guide to Surviving

MODERN TECHNOLOGY

Rights Reserved Statement

Disclaimer

This book is intended to entertain and provide a humorous take on modern technology. If you find yourself excessively grumpy while navigating the digital age, just remember it's all in good fun—unless your smart assistant starts talking back. The author assumes no responsibility for any "rage-quitting" of devices, accidental yelling at inanimate objects, or sudden urges to throw your smartphone out the window. Laugh, roll your eyes, and keep calm—it's only technology, after all.

Table of Contents

Introduction: "Technology Was Supposed to Make This Easier!"

Remember when life was simpler? When a phone was something that hung on a wall, and the most challenging tech you had to figure out was the VCR clock? Those were the good old days. Now, everything around us—from our lightbulbs to our fridges—wants to be "smart," and it's left us feeling a little bit, well, dumb.

Welcome to *The Grumpy Old Man's Guide to Surviving Modern Technology*. If you've ever struggled with your smartphone's baffling updates, felt personally attacked by an emoji, or wondered why on Earth you need an app to operate your toaster, this guide is for you. We'll dive headfirst into the chaotic mess of gadgets, apps, and digital nonsense that's supposed to make our lives easier but often ends up being a major headache. From battling the confusing settings of smart thermostats to figuring out why your smartwatch thinks you need to take more steps while you're just trying to relax, we're going to cover it all. Expect plenty of grumbling, a few minor victories, and lots of relatable frustration.

Think of this book as your survival guide through the madness—full of rants, relatable moments, and maybe a bit of hard-won wisdom. I'm not here to sugarcoat it —technology can be frustrating, confusing, and sometimes downright maddening. We'll rant about the absurdity of voice assistants, tackle the madness of endless app permissions, and maybe even find some humor in our struggles along the way. Together, we're going to laugh, roll our eyes, and uncover the small victories hiding amidst all the technological chaos. So grab your reading glasses (if you can still find them), put your phone on silent, and let's embark on this journey of grumpy tech survival.

Smartphones: "A Smarter Phone Than Its Owner?"

Ah, smartphones. Those tiny devices that supposedly make our lives more efficient but often leave us more confused than a dog watching a card trick. Once upon a time, a phone was just a phone—something you picked up to call someone, or hung up when you'd had enough. Now? It's a camera, a calculator, a fitness coach, a notepad, a map, a digital wallet, and an alarm clock, all wrapped into one shiny, headache-inducing package. And let's not forget the occasional role of therapist, when we find ourselves ranting at it for yet another failed feature.

Have you ever tried unlocking your phone with facial recognition after just rolling out of bed? The device doesn't even know who you are, as if you've undergone a radical overnight transformation—perhaps from a coherent adult to a blurry-eyed creature straight out of a horror movie. Or maybe you've attempted to use voice commands, only to have your phone misinterpret "play jazz music" as "call Jan's ex." Now you're stuck in a confusing conversation with someone you haven't thought about in years, all because Siri or Google Assistant decided to improvise. And don't even get me started on the constant stream of notifications. Every app thinks it's more important than your best friend, bombarding you with updates, messages, and reminders you never asked for. Suddenly, your phone feels less like a helpful assistant and more like a needy toddler pulling at your pant leg every few seconds, begging for attention.

Then there's the lovely adventure of software updates. Just when you've finally figured out where everything is and how it works, your phone decides it's time for an "improvement." Suddenly, icons are missing, the layout is all different, and the simple swipe you used to do to get to your messages now opens some obscure new feature that you didn't even know you had. And let's not forget the ongoing storage battle. One minute you're taking a cute picture of your dog, and the next, you're hit with the dreaded "Storage Full" notification. So now it's a choice between deleting photos of your grandkids or that overly large app you haven't used since 2019.

Smartphones. They promise to be our loyal sidekicks, our pocket-sized geniuses ready to make life a breeze. But are they really that smart? Sometimes it feels like they're just here to complicate things—like a wannabe know-it-all who's great at showing off but falls short when you actually need them. Take, for example, the infamous "other" category in your phone's storage. It's that dark, enigmatic section of the storage graph that somehow consumes half of your device's space. You swipe through your photos, delete apps you haven't opened since 2017, and yet, that mysterious "other" keeps expanding, like some kind of digital blob that feeds on your sanity. It leaves you wondering if it's storing old secrets, outdated software, or perhaps all those selfies that failed so badly your phone decided they should be put away forever.

And let's be honest—are the constant software updates meant to help us or just drive us crazy? Nothing is more irritating than your phone cheerfully reminding you, "Update available!" Oh really? I was just getting used to where all my buttons were, thank you very much! One moment you've got your favorite apps organized just how you like them, and the next, you wake up to a device that looks entirely different, almost like it's been rearranging itself while you were asleep. Your trusty swipe to open your messages now launches a random game you didn't even know you had, and there's a new feature you never asked for but apparently cannot avoid. It's almost as if your phone thrives on chaos, determined to keep you on your toes.

Then we have the dreaded autocorrect—no conversation about smartphone annoyances would be complete without it. It's as if it has a sixth sense for when you're trying to be professional or sincere, and that's exactly when it strikes. You write, "I'm looking forward to the meeting," but it decides "I'm lurking forward to the melting" would be better. Suddenly, you've sent off a message that makes you sound either like a comic book villain or someone desperately in need of air conditioning. Autocorrect always seems to delight in making you look just ridiculous enough that you can't ignore it, but not so much that it becomes obvious. You might even call it a quiet saboteur.

And of course, there's privacy. Why does every app feel entitled to your personal life? You just want to check the weather, but before you can do that, the app requests access to your location, your photos, your microphone, and possibly your mother's maiden name. It's ridiculous! You sit there, looking at a weather app, thinking, "I just want to know if I need an umbrella, not whether I need to call in cybersecurity." The more apps you download, the more you realize that your phone isn't just a handy tool—it's a suspiciously nosy assistant, logging your every move and politely pretending it's all for your convenience.

Grumpy's Tips for Surviving Smartphones

- **Turn Off Notifications (Yes, All of Them)**

Go through each app's settings and silence anything unnecessary. You don't need a ping every time someone likes your cousin's vacation photo. Declutter your mind by muting the madness. Only keep essential notifications on—like those reminding you where you left your car.

- **Face Unlock is a Gamble—Stick with the Passcode**

Unless you enjoy being unrecognized by your own phone at 6 a.m., ditch facial recognition. A trusty passcode or fingerprint sensor will save you from countless awkward attempts to make your phone understand that yes, it really is you, even if you're half-asleep.

- **Autocorrect is Not Your Friend**

Double-check every message before you hit "send." Autocorrect has a mind of its own, and that mind often enjoys chaos. If you can, turn it off and trust your own typing skills—even if they're not perfect, at least you know you won't be accidentally threatening to "lurk" at an office party.

Grumpy's Tips for Surviving Smartphones

- **Beware of the "Other" Storage Gremlin**

The "other" category in your storage will never make sense. Accept it. Make it a monthly ritual to delete old videos, unused apps, and anything remotely suspicious. Think of it as spring-cleaning for your digital life— without the dust but with just as much frustration.

- **Ignore the Constant Updates**

Unless it's a critical security update, resist the urge to hit "Update Now." They always come at the worst times, and half the time they seem to make things worse rather than better. Stick to updating once every few months, and enjoy the predictability while it lasts.

- **Be Wary of App Permissions**

The next time a flashlight app asks for permission to access your contacts, just say no. There's no reason that checking the weather should require permission to listen in on your conversations. Review app permissions and revoke anything that seems more nosy than necessary.

Grumpy's Tips for Surviving Smartphones

- **Organize Your Home Screen for Sanity**

Cut down on the chaos. Keep your most-used apps on the home screen and hide everything else. Better yet, delete anything that hasn't seen use in a year. Your phone doesn't need to look like a cluttered junk drawer —keep it simple and practical, and save yourself some scrolling.

- **Put the Phone Down**

Remember, the best way to deal with smartphone headaches is to step away from them. Put the phone in another room, take a walk, or just stare out the window for a while. You managed just fine without a mini-computer attached to your hand before, and you can do it again—at least for an hour or two.

By following these tips, you can reclaim a little control from your "smart" phone and hopefully save yourself from the digital madness. Remember, the less your phone runs your life, the less grumpy you'll feel about it.

Social Media Madness: "Why Do I Need to Like Your Breakfast?"

Ah, social media—the place where everyone you've ever met decides to share every waking moment, and a few non-waking ones too. Once upon a time, breakfast was just something you ate, quietly, without an audience. Now, thanks to the internet, Brad from high school thinks the world needs to know he's having avocado toast for the third morning in a row. And not just know it—you're supposed to like it, maybe even comment on it. Because in the age of social media, nothing is real until someone else gives it a thumbs-up.

And it's not just breakfast. Social media demands we share everything—where we've been, who we were with, what we were doing, and how we were feeling at every single moment. Forget about keeping up with the Joneses; now you're supposed to keep up with the filtered, hashtagged version of everyone's lives that makes you wonder if you're the one missing out. Your friends are off on tropical vacations while you're sitting on your worn-out sofa, scrolling, and feeling like maybe, just maybe, you need a break—from social media.

Don't get me wrong, there are times when it's useful. Want to reconnect with a long-lost cousin? Need to know where the best pizza in town is, according to 300 strangers? Social media's got you. But it also comes with endless notifications. "New friend suggestion!" "Your friend's mom liked a page called 'Knitting for Cats'!" Great, but why do I need to know that? And why does my phone keep buzzing, demanding I take notice of every little thing happening in other people's lives? Somewhere along the way, we blurred the line between important information and pointless noise, until everything became an endless stream of updates you could easily live without.

The worst part of it all? The algorithms that decide what you should see. Interact with one cat meme, and suddenly your entire feed is cats. Not just any cats— cats in hats, cats in sweaters, cats performing Broadway musicals. And heaven forbid you linger too long on an ad for orthopedic shoes—you'll be getting recommendations for compression socks for the next month. It's like the algorithms have a mind of their own, insisting you need more of exactly what you're already tired of. At the end of the day, you either laugh or you go mad.

Social media is supposed to connect us, but sometimes it just makes us feel more disconnected. Scrolling through picture-perfect lives, seeing everyone's highlight reels, it's easy to forget that behind every photo is someone else just as bored, tired, and fed up as you are. So why do we keep logging in? Maybe it's FOMO (that's "Fear of Missing Out" for anyone who's not fluent in internet slang). Maybe it's the hope of finding something that makes you genuinely smile. Or maybe, just maybe, we enjoy a good rant now and then. Whatever the reason, social media is here to stay, and it's up to us to navigate its madness—preferably with a sense of humor, a healthy dose of skepticism, and the occasional log-off for our sanity.

Grumpy's Tips for Surviving Social Media Madness

- **Limit Scrolling Time**

Set a timer when you hop onto social media. Thirty minutes tops, then put the phone down. If you want to maintain your sanity, limit the time you spend scrolling through avocado toasts and vacation snapshots.

- **Curate Ruthlessly**

Unfollow accounts that make you roll your eyes or compare your life to theirs. Just because someone insists on posting about their workouts doesn't mean you need to be their audience. Keep only what adds value or genuine joy.

- **Turn Off Notifications**

Go into your settings and turn off as many notifications as possible. You don't need a ping every time someone likes Brad's breakfast post or shares a meme. Silence the noise—your mental peace will thank you.

Grumpy's Tips for Surviving Social Media Madness

- **Resist the "Like" Pressure**

Not everything deserves a thumbs-up. It's okay not to "like" someone's soggy cereal or a blurry picture of their dog. A world where you only "like" the genuinely interesting things is a much better one.

- **Mute Group Chats**

Those massive group chats can quickly become overwhelming with dozens of people all chiming in. Mute them, check them at your own pace, and don't feel bad if you don't respond to every "LOL." It's your sanity at stake.

- **Remember, It's Not Real**

Nobody's life is as glamorous as their social media makes it seem. Behind every tropical vacation photo is someone stressed about lost luggage, and behind every smiling selfie is a dozen outtakes. Keep perspective— it's a curated version of reality, not the whole truth.

Grumpy's Tips for Surviving Social Media Madness

- **Log Off Now and Then**

You don't need to be online 24/7. It's perfectly okay to take breaks—long ones, even. Go outside, read a book, talk to a real person, or just stare at the sky. Your mental health will thank you, and you'll realize life offline isn't so bad.

- **Embrace the Chaos**

Algorithms are weird, and there's no perfect way to game them. If you see too many cat memes, maybe you just need to laugh at it. Don't let the madness get to you. Embrace it, have a chuckle, and remember you can always scroll past.

Social media is a tool—it can be fun, useful, and yes, maddening. The trick is making sure you're the one in control, not the app on your phone. Stay grumpy, stay selective, and don't be afraid to log off when it's all too much.

Streaming Overload: "How Many Subscriptions Does It Take to Watch One Show?"

Remember the days when you could just flip on the TV, tune into one of five available channels, and there it was—entertainment? Sure, you had to sit through a few ads about shampoo or soap powder, but at least everything was in one place, and you knew where to find it. Fast forward to today, and suddenly we need an Excel spreadsheet just to keep track of where our favorite shows are playing. If it's not Netflix, then it's Amazon Prime. If it's not on Amazon, it's Hulu. Or maybe it's Disney+. Or Apple TV+. Or Peacock. Or HBO Max. Honestly, it feels like you need a subscription to some secret, exclusive club just to watch a sitcom that ended ten years ago.

Streaming services are supposed to make life easier— no more scheduled TV slots, no more recording on VHS tapes, no more hunting for a good movie on a Saturday night. Instead, they've made life feel like a scavenger hunt with absolutely zero clues. Want to watch that new hit drama everyone is raving about? Oh, it's on "Random New Streaming Service XYZ." Never heard of it? Well, they only have the one show you care about, so fork over $9.99 a month for the privilege of being in the know. But wait, you already pay for six other streaming services, each nibbling away at your wallet like a colony of very greedy termites. And, of course, the second you decide to cancel one because you're tired of paying for shows you never watch, you discover that your favorite comfort show—the one you put on to unwind after a long day—has migrated over there, meaning it's time to sign back up.

And let's not forget the endless scrolling. Thousands of shows, documentaries, movies, and "original" content to choose from, and yet, somehow, there's nothing to watch. You sit down, remote in hand, ready to relax, only to find yourself paralyzed by an endless wall of thumbnails and overly enthusiastic descriptions. You might think you're about to watch a heartwarming romantic comedy, only to realize halfway through that it's a dark psychological thriller about an unhinged florist. Or, worse yet, you end up spending an hour just browsing through titles, eventually landing on something you've seen a dozen times because deciding is just too much work. Who knew having too many options could be just as frustrating as having none at all?

Then there's the autoplay feature—the thing that seems to be on a mission to rob us all of sleep. You finish one episode, the credits barely roll, and suddenly you're two minutes into the next. You know you should probably stop, maybe head to bed like a responsible adult, but Netflix has other plans. It slyly counts down from five, and before you know it, you're deep into another episode and whispering to yourself, "Just one more." It's like the service knows your weakness, preying on your inability to say no to cliffhangers. It's a never-ending cycle of binge-watching, sleeplessness, and guilt.

And what's with the content wars? It's like the streaming services are all kids on the playground fighting over who gets to keep the good toys. One month, all your favorite sitcoms are available in one convenient spot. The next month, they're scattered across four different services, each one demanding a separate subscription. The second you finally get comfortable and know where to find your favorite show, it gets yoinked away and handed over to a rival service. And don't even get me started on the rotating availability of movies. That classic action flick you've been wanting to rewatch? Well, it was available last week, but now it's been snatched away, probably hiding behind a new paywall. It's like playing hide and seek with your entertainment—except no one's having fun.

In the good old days of cable TV, you had a few hundred channels that mostly played reruns and infomercials, but at least you weren't chasing individual shows across a labyrinth of subscription services. Now, you need to remember passwords, subscription fees, and which of your friends might still have that HBO password you borrowed a year ago. The modern TV experience has somehow managed to be both overly convenient and endlessly frustrating at the same time. We've gone from shouting at our TV remotes to shouting at log-in screens, and I'm not entirely convinced it's an upgrade.

Grumpy's Tips for Surviving Streaming Overload

- **Simplify**

Cancel the services you don't watch. You don't need all of them all the time. Rotate through the subscriptions based on what shows you want to see—finish a series, then move on to the next service.

- **Set Boundaries**

Limit your screen time Autoplay is sneaky, so turn it off if you can. Stick to a reasonable number of episodes per night—your future, well-rested self will thank you.

- **Embrace the Classics**

Sometimes, the best entertainment is what you already own. Dust off those old DVDs or even VHS tapes if you have them. No subscriptions, no scrolling, just good old-fashioned entertainment.

- **Password Organization**

Keep track of your subscriptions and passwords. Write them down, use a password manager, or bribe your tech-savvy niece to help you out.

- **Go Old-School**

Take a deep breath and turn off the TV altogether. Grab a book, play a board game, or just enjoy the silence. Sometimes, the best escape from streaming overload is to not stream at all.

Endless Software Updates: "Didn't I Just Update This Thing Yesterday?"

Ah, the dreaded software updates—those pesky pop-up messages that seem to strike at the most inconvenient moments. Just when you sit down to use your phone or computer, there it is: "Update available." These notifications are relentless. It's as if your devices have decided to take up a hobby—only their hobby is testing your patience, one update at a time.

It's almost comical how often it happens. You just finished updating your phone, and the next day, here comes another one. It's as if the tech companies are in a race to see who can release the most updates in a single year. "New features," they say, "Bug fixes," they promise. But honestly, how many bugs could there possibly be? And why does it feel like every update just makes the device more confusing? One minute, all your icons are exactly where you like them, and after the update, you're playing a game of digital hide-and-seek to find your own apps.

The most infuriating part of these updates is how vague they are. "General improvements and bug fixes," they claim. What bugs? What improvements? Sometimes you just want specifics—like, "We fixed the bug that made your phone call your ex whenever you tried to dial your mother" or "We've made sure the weather app stops predicting snow in July." Instead, they leave us in the dark, as if we're supposed to just trust that this mysterious update is for our own good.

And let's not forget the dreaded moment when an update breaks something that wasn't broken. You know, the type of update that leaves your favorite app crashing every time you open it or makes your once-smooth phone feel like it's running on hamster power. It's like the tech companies are saying, "Remember that thing you liked about your phone? Yeah, we changed it for no reason." Sometimes, you wish they'd just leave well enough alone.

If the frequency isn't enough to drive you mad, the timing certainly is. Why do updates always demand your attention just when you need to use your device? It's like they wait for the exact moment you're in a rush to send an email or make a call. "Please install this update now," it insists, as if your urgent meeting or dinner reservation isn't important. And heaven forbid you hit "Remind me later"—because "later" just means "every hour until you finally cave in."

The best part of all? The mandatory restarts. Yes, because there's nothing better than waiting for your computer to slowly power down, install the update, and then restart while you stare at the ceiling and wonder why you ever clicked "Update" in the first place. It's especially delightful when your device decides to update itself in the middle of the night, and you wake up to find it halfway through an installation, with no idea when you'll be able to use it again.

Grumpy's Tips for Surviving Endless Software Updates

- **Ignore Until Necessary**

Unless something is broken, there's no rush to update. Most of the time, waiting a bit means fewer bugs and less frustration.

- **Schedule Updates**

If you must update, schedule it for a time when you won't need your device—like when you're asleep (assuming it doesn't decide to update itself three times in a row).

- **Turn Off Auto-Update**

For apps, turn off automatic updates. You don't need your favorite game changing its layout overnight without warning. Update on your own terms.

- **Read the Fine Print**

Before updating, read the release notes. At least you'll have a vague idea of what's coming, even if it's just "bug fixes" and "performance enhancements."

- **Backup Regularly**

Before any major software update, make sure to back up your data. You never know when an "improvement" might lead to an unexpected crash.

The Emoji Epidemic: "Emojis Are Not Real Words, People!"

Remember when language was just about, you know, words? Those good old days when communication involved carefully chosen phrases or, at the very least, full sentences? Well, that's all gone out the window thanks to the Emoji Epidemic. Now, instead of meaningful conversation, we have small digital doodles that somehow are expected to convey everything from love to sarcasm to full-blown existential crises. Emojis, folks—they're not real words. But try telling that to the world today.

Let's be clear here: emojis were supposed to be a fun addition, a little garnish on the entrée of our language. Instead, they've become the main course. We used to write, "I'm feeling a bit under the weather today." Now it's all " 😷 💤 😴 ," and everyone just nods knowingly, as if three little pictographs are somehow better than spelling out your misery in real, actual language. And don't even get me started on the people who try to have entire conversations in emoji. I got a text the other day that was just a random sequence of fire, thumbs up, crying-laughing face, and a panda. What am I supposed to do with that? Is it a compliment? A distress call? An invitation to join a secret cult? Who knows?

The most frustrating thing about the Emoji Epidemic is that people have forgotten how to use their words. It's like we've reverted to a more primitive version of humanity—hieroglyphics, but with more eggplants and smiling turds. You can send a message today that simply reads "😂🏠😷" and people will think you've just written the next great piece of literature. It's even worse when you get emojis that are clearly meant to soften the blow of something awful. Imagine getting a text from your boss that reads, "We need to talk. 😬" Oh, great! You've softened the impending doom with an awkward face. Everything's fine now. I feel so much better about getting fired.

And then there's the overuse of emojis in professional settings, which is a true horror show. I once received an email about an important deadline, and it ended with "Let's crush it! 💪🚀." I'm sorry, but if you want me to meet a deadline, don't add a rocket emoji. It doesn't make me feel motivated—it makes me want to roll my eyes so hard that I can see the back of my own brain. We're supposed to be professionals here, not enthusiastic camp counselors trying to hype everyone up for a marshmallow roast.

What's really baffling is how emojis can mean different things to different people. A winking face might mean "I'm joking" to some, while to others it's "I'm flirting," and to a select few, it's "I've just committed a terrible crime but let's keep it between us." There's no standardization, and that's the real issue. At least with words, we mostly all agree on what they mean. But with emojis, it's like everyone's just making it up as they go. That little peach emoji? Let's be honest—it's not about fruit. We all know it. The double hands up in the air? Sometimes it's "hallelujah," other times it's "I give up." It's exhausting.

And speaking of the infamous eggplant and peach, when did we decide that grocery produce was the best way to represent our most intimate thoughts? I mean, really—this is where we are now? A proud civilization capable of splitting atoms and landing on the moon, but we've reduced flirting to sending vegetables and fruits? My grandparents used love letters, long heartfelt declarations on carefully chosen stationery. Today, we're just chucking an eggplant at someone and hoping they get the hint. Progress, right?

Look, I'm not saying we need to go full emoji prohibition here. They do have their moments—they can add some flair to an otherwise dull message or let someone know that yes, you are indeed being sarcastic.

A well-placed laughing face or thumbs-up can go a long way in a light-hearted conversation. But can we at least agree to keep them as a supplement, not the main course?

They're like sprinkles on the communication cake, not the entire dessert. Emojis aren't a substitute for real language. They shouldn't be the backbone of our communication, but rather an occasional quirky addition to emphasize a point. If you're relying solely on little cartoon images to express the entirety of your feelings, it might be time to revisit how words actually work.

Because, believe me, the next time I see someone trying to communicate complex emotions solely through a string of random pictographs, I'm sending them the biggest, most emphatic facepalm emoji I can find—and yes, that will be drenched in irony.

Grumpy's Tips for Surviving the Emoji Epidemic

- **Use Words First**

If you have something important to say, use actual words. Emojis are for emphasis, not for substance. Don't expect a tiny cartoon to carry the weight of your heartfelt messages.

- **Avoid Emojis in Professional Settings**

Unless you work at a summer camp or in a sticker factory, keep the emojis out of work emails. No one needs a smiley face at the end of a memo about budget cuts.

- **Be Clear About Your Intentions**

If you must use an emoji, make sure it's clear. Avoid ambiguity—if there's even a chance someone might misinterpret your peach, find another way to say what you mean.

- **Don't Replace Sentences with Emojis**

A crying-laughing face is not a substitute for actually explaining why something is funny. Words exist for a reason—don't be afraid to use them.

In conclusion, emojis are like spices—use them well and they add flavor. Overdo it, and suddenly no one knows what they're eating anymore. Let's bring back actual language, one less eggplant at a time.

Digital Assistants: "Stop Talking to Me, Alexa!"

Remember when you used to walk into a room, flip a switch, and voilà—the lights turned on? Simple, effective, and nobody talked back to you. Now, we live in an age where even our lightbulbs need Wi-Fi, and worse, where devices think they should chime in on our conversations. Enter Alexa, Google Assistant, Siri, and whatever other digital nosy-parkers are out there. Digital assistants promised convenience but ended up becoming those annoying roommates who never know when to be quiet or just outright ignore you when you actually need them.

It all begins with the promise: "Just ask Alexa, and she'll do it for you." She'll play your favorite song, tell you the weather, remind you to pick up eggs, or, in theory, answer any question you throw at her. But what no one tells you is that for every moment of convenience, you'll get twice the headache. Like that one time I asked Alexa to play some jazz, and she decided that I must want a deep dive into some obscure experimental death metal instead. I didn't ask for a soundtrack to an existential crisis, but there it was, blaring at full volume. Nothing like a bit of atonal chaos to accompany your morning coffee.

And why, oh why, are they always listening? You're chatting with a friend about taking a vacation, and suddenly Alexa lights up, uninvited, and starts recommending flights to the Bahamas. No one asked for your input, Alexa! It's like having that one friend who eavesdrops and then jumps in at all the wrong times. Only worse, because this "friend" is wired into the internet, ready to offer flight deals, dinner recipes, and incorrect trivia at the drop of a hat. I didn't know what it felt like to be spied on by a digital butler, and frankly, I could've lived my whole life without knowing.

Let's talk about their peculiar sense of humor, or lack thereof. I mean, try asking Siri a joke, and you'll be lucky if you get something even mildly amusing. "Why did the chicken cross the road? To avoid being asked pointless questions by humans." Gee, thanks for that, Siri. Really cutting-edge comedy right there. It's as if they're taking subtle digs at us for needing their help in the first place. Imagine a regular assistant giving you that kind of sass—they'd be out the door faster than you could say "you're fired." But not Siri or Alexa. We just sigh, nod, and carry on, while they secretly revel in their glitchy superiority.

The most infuriating part? They never quite understand you when it actually matters. It's a roll of the dice whether they'll get it right. You say, "Alexa, turn off the living room lights," and she replies, "I'm sorry, I didn't quite catch that. Would you like me to add 'living room delights' to your shopping list?" No, Alexa, I don't need more delight—I need darkness. Yet, ask her something absolutely irrelevant like, "How many stars are in the galaxy?" and suddenly she's the universe's foremost astrophysicist, listing facts faster than you can blink. It's as if she's trolling us—intentionally efficient about the things we don't care about, but willfully obtuse when it comes to anything practical.

And the worst part—the routines. Oh, the routines! You set them up, thinking you're some kind of futuristic genius who'll finally have a smart home that works seamlessly. "Alexa, set a bedtime routine: dim the lights, turn on calming music, lower the thermostat." Easy, right? Wrong. Suddenly, the thermostat is in tropical mode, the lights are flashing like you're at a disco, and instead of calming music, Alexa has decided it's time for a podcast about true crime. Nothing like stories of murder to lull you into a restful sleep, right?

Then there's the fear that maybe, just maybe, Alexa knows too much. She's always there, always listening. Sure, they say she only activates with the "wake word," but isn't it funny how she always seems to know when I'm talking about buying something? Suddenly, my ads are full of air fryers because I mentioned it in passing while talking to my spouse. Coincidence? I think not. It's like having a nosy relative who's always eavesdropping and then drops "subtle" hints based on everything you said when you thought no one was listening. I can almost hear Alexa whispering, "Oh, I heard you mention air fryers. Would you like me to recommend the top five?"

So here's the truth—digital assistants aren't exactly making our lives stress-free. If anything, they're just adding another layer of frustration to a world that's already pretty good at making us want to scream. They're part convenience, part nuisance, and part uninvited spy. We tolerate them because, every now and then, they actually do what they're supposed to—but never without a few glitches and a healthy dose of sarcasm.

Grumpy's Top Tips for Dealing with Digital Assistants

- **Use the Mute Button**

If Alexa or Google gets too chatty, just mute them. It's the closest thing you'll get to putting them in time-out.

- **Stick to Basic Commands**

Don't get fancy. The simpler the request, the less likely they'll misinterpret it and add "alpaca grooming kits" to your shopping list.

- **Turn Off Purchase Permissions**

Trust me, you don't want a digital assistant buying things for you. It's only a matter of time before you end up with a bulk order of something ridiculous, like 50 pounds of catnip.

- **Reset Expectations**

Accept that digital assistants are about 40% helpful, 40% frustrating, and 20% creepy. Keep your expectations low, and you might just avoid losing your mind.

- **Keep Personal Conversations Far Away**

If it's personal, take it elsewhere. The last thing you need is Alexa chiming in during a heart-to-heart to offer you a deal on tissues.

So next time Alexa decides to offer unsolicited advice or completely ignore a straightforward command, just remember—she might be "smart," but she's still far from perfect. And maybe, just maybe, it's time we all learn to appreciate the good old-fashioned light switch again.

Privacy Woes: "Who Told My Phone I Needed New Socks?"

Do you ever get the feeling that your phone knows a little too much about you? Maybe you were just chatting with a friend about needing new socks, and suddenly, your screen is plastered with ads for cozy woolen wonders. It's as if your phone has ears—scratch that, it definitely has ears—and it's taking notes on your every whim and desire. Forget Big Brother, folks—it's your own pocket-sized sidekick that's doing all the spying.

Let's be honest. In the good old days, privacy meant something entirely different. You could mumble under your breath about needing a new toaster, and the only response you'd get was maybe a raised eyebrow from the family pet. Fast forward to today: mention a simple household item within earshot of your smartphone, and boom—you've got fifty ads and a coupon for toasters at a store you didn't even know existed. It's like living in an infomercial, except you didn't ask to be part of the audience.

And it's not just ads. You know that little feature that tracks your location "to help improve your experience"? Let's call it what it really is—an excuse for your phone to know exactly where you are, all the time. Once, I tried turning off the location settings, but then my phone insisted it could no longer tell me the weather, help with directions, or even set an alarm correctly. It's almost as if these devices are holding us hostage: let us spy on you, or enjoy a smartphone that's only useful as a very overpriced paperweight.

Ever had a conversation that felt like it led to a completely nonsensical ad? Like you're discussing your favorite dinosaur with your nephew, and suddenly, there's an ad in your feed for a "Velociraptor-Themed Birthday Bash"? I don't even have kids, but apparently, my phone thinks I need raptor-themed party favors. It's moments like this that make you wonder if our phones are genuinely listening, or if there's some secret algorithm that's so smart it's practically clairvoyant. Either way, it's equal parts impressive and unsettling.

Then there's the endless demand for permissions. You want to download a simple flashlight app? Great, except that it apparently needs access to your camera, microphone, and personal contacts. Why does a flashlight need to know who my emergency contact is? Are they worried I'll get trapped in a dark room and need to call Aunt Margie to come save me? It's either that, or this innocent app is the Trojan horse of data collection, here to pilfer every bit of personal information it can. Frankly, I'm betting on the latter.

We've also got the problem of "helpful" reminders. It's bad enough that my phone knows I have a dentist appointment next week, but now it's also trying to suggest socks to keep my feet warm on the way there. It's like living with a digital assistant that's part personal shopper, part nagging parent. "Don't forget your dentist appointment... also, have you considered buying some new athletic socks to help with that brisk morning walk?" Thanks, phone. If I wanted fashion advice, I'd probably get it from literally anywhere else.

At the end of the day, we're all stuck in this privacy nightmare together. Our devices know where we go, what we like, and apparently, what kind of socks we need. Privacy used to be about keeping your secrets safe, but in the digital age, it seems like the goal is just to make sure your secrets don't get sold to the highest bidder. We might not be able to stop our gadgets from listening, but we can definitely gripe about it—and maybe laugh a little while we're at it.

Grumpy's Tips for Surviving Privacy Woes

- **Turn Off What You Don't Need**

Go into your phone settings and shut off permissions for apps that have no business knowing where you are. A calculator doesn't need to know your location—don't give it the chance.

- **Read Before You Tap**

Before you mindlessly tap "Allow," take a second and ask yourself, "Does this app really need to access my photos?" If the answer is no, hit deny. It's the small victories that count.

- **Incognito Browsing**

Use private browsing when looking up sensitive things. If nothing else, at least it'll make it a bit harder for those ads to chase you around the internet like a needy ex.

- **Disable the Mic**

If you don't use voice commands often, turn off the microphone for as many apps as possible. The fewer apps that can listen in, the fewer chances they have to surprise you with creepy, ultra-specific ads.

- **Accept Imperfection**

Just accept that your phone is always going to know too much. The sooner we come to terms with the fact that privacy is a bygone era, the sooner we can at least have a good chuckle at the absurdity of it all.

In the end, privacy in the digital age is like a mythical unicorn—something everyone talks about but no one has ever actually seen. We've gone from secrets whispered in confidence to ads that seem to know we want socks before we do. Whether it's your flashlight app trying to get into your contacts or your phone playing detective on your shopping habits, there's no escaping the surveillance. So, embrace the absurdity, laugh at the chaos, and remember—if your phone knows you need new socks, at least it's trying to be helpful, right? Sort of.

Modern Etiquette: "Stop Texting When We're Having Dinner!"

Ah, dinner—once a sacred ritual, now a battleground in the war of the screens. There was a time when dinner was a chance to sit down, unwind, and genuinely connect with the people around you. But nowadays, it seems more like an exercise in seeing whose screen can light up the fastest. Nothing says "quality time" quite like trying to have a conversation while your dinner partner is busy typing away, one thumb at a time, to tell someone else what they're having for dinner.

Honestly, when did it become acceptable to answer a text while someone is pouring their heart out across the table? Imagine you're sharing a story, pouring out the details, only to look up and see that your friend is distracted, tapping furiously to tell Sarah about that "cute dog video" they just saw. We've all been there—mid-sentence, only to be cut off by the dreaded ping of a notification. It's not just rude; it's a declaration that the moment you're sharing is apparently less exciting than Karen's new throw pillows.

And don't even get me started on the social media enthusiasts—the ones who need to snap a photo of every single meal, sometimes before you even have a chance to take a bite. Are you really enjoying that plate of spaghetti if you're busy angling for the perfect shot with just the right amount of steam? Trust me, no one is scrolling Instagram thinking, "I hope I get to see Jim's mashed potatoes tonight." Let's put the camera down and pick up the fork, shall we?

The thing is, people seem to have forgotten that phones are supposed to be tools—not substitutes for real-life interactions. They might connect us to the world, but they disconnect us from the moment we're in. How many important details have we all missed because we were too busy staring at our glowing little rectangles? Eye contact used to be a sign of respect, but now, you'd think we're all just trying to avoid it at all costs, as if our eyes might accidentally catch on fire if they stray too far from our screens.

And it's not just about the phones, either. It's about the constant need to be somewhere else—mentally, if not physically. It's like people are terrified of fully engaging in the present moment, afraid that they might actually have to, you know, participate. Maybe it's a defense mechanism—if we pretend we're busy enough, we don't have to deal with awkward pauses, real feelings, or the horrifying thought of silence. But hey, a little awkward silence never killed anyone. Unlike a text-heavy dinner, it might even help us learn more about each other.

So, the next time you're at a dinner, here's an idea: leave your phone in your pocket. Better yet, leave it in the car. The world can wait, and so can Sarah's new throw pillows. Dinner is for connecting—with the people right in front of you, not for "liking" the latest photo of someone else's plate. Let's make dinner time about actual face time. And remember, no matter how clever your friend thinks they are, the only proper response to a dinner conversation isn't "LOL."

Grumpy's Top Tips for Surviving Dinner with a Phone Addict

- **The Phone Basket**

Make it a rule—phones go in a basket until the end of the meal. Out of sight, out of mind, and certainly out of reach of any tempting ping.

- **Airplane Mode**

Just accept that your phone is always going to know too much. The sooner we come to terms with the fact that privacy is a bygone era, the sooner we can at least have a good chuckle at the absurdity of it all.

- **The 10-Minute Rule**

Allow ten minutes at the start of the meal to handle anything urgent on your phone. After that, it's a screen-free zone. If it's still on your mind after that, maybe you need a new hobby.

- **Set the Example**

Keep your own phone away. It's hard to argue for a phone-free dinner if you're sneakily checking the score of the game under the table. Practice what you preach, and maybe—just maybe—others will follow suit.

Let's bring the good old days of dinners back—where the only distraction was a bit of spilt gravy, not someone's incessant need to scroll through their phone. If we can put a man on the moon, surely we can have a meal without a notification frenzy.

Cryptocurrency: Investing in Invisible Money

Cryptocurrency—let's talk about it. It's the magical digital money that apparently has everyone and their cousin convinced they're going to get rich without ever leaving their couch. Don't get me wrong, I'm all for a good old-fashioned get-rich-quick scheme, but something about investing in invisible coins just doesn't sit right with me. Call me old-fashioned, but I prefer to actually see my money, even if it's just a few sad bills in my wallet. With crypto, all you get are numbers on a screen, and a lot of promises that, frankly, sound like a scammer's dream.

First off, let's address the elephant in the room: Bitcoin. The original cryptocurrency, the big cheese, the one everyone talks about like it's some mystical treasure. Except instead of gold doubloons hidden in a chest, you've got strings of computer code and a vague hope that it might be worth something tomorrow. And let's be real, the price of Bitcoin swings more wildly than my mood when I discover my favorite TV show's been cancelled. One day it's skyrocketing, the next it's tanking, and meanwhile, people are either declaring themselves millionaires or drowning their sorrows in bargain whiskey because their "investment" vanished overnight.

And it's not just Bitcoin anymore. Oh no, now we have Ethereum, Dogecoin, Shiba Inu, and a dozen other coins named after adorable dogs. I mean, Dogecoin started as a joke, and somehow people are now betting their life savings on it. I thought my generation was risky with some of our choices, but apparently "investing" in a meme about a Shiba Inu takes the cake. I suppose it's fitting—nothing says modern life quite like putting your financial future in the paws of an internet-famous dog.

Let's also touch on the phenomenon of crypto wallets. Not an actual wallet, mind you—no leather, no compartments, no trusty zipper. No, a crypto wallet is a piece of software that lets you access your magical invisible coins. They say these wallets are secure, but I've read too many stories about people forgetting their passwords and losing millions. Imagine: you invested your hard-earned cash, watched it grow, and suddenly you can't remember your password because it was some complicated combination like "45Ftg!9$%LmnopJ8." And no, there's no nice bank teller to help you recover it—you're just out of luck. Your invisible money is now gone forever, floating somewhere in the digital ether, laughing at your inability to remember that last special character.

Then there's NFTs—those "non-fungible tokens." Essentially, you're buying a digital receipt to prove you "own" something that exists only online. Want to buy a cartoon monkey? Sure, here's a drawing and a receipt for it, and that'll be a few thousand dollars, please. I don't know about you, but if I'm spending that kind of cash, I want something I can put on my wall, not a glorified JPEG I have to explain to people. The only token I understand is the kind that used to get me a ride on the subway, and it was a heck of a lot more useful than an NFT.

And let's not forget the environmental impact of this whole mess. All that mining requires a ludicrous amount of energy. Back in my day, if someone said they were mining, I'd picture a guy with a pickaxe, not a warehouse full of computers consuming enough electricity to power a small country. It's like we're trying to destroy the planet faster, all for the sake of chasing invisible money that might just disappear in the blink of an eye. Brilliant, really.

Look, if you want to get involved in cryptocurrency, more power to you. Maybe you'll strike it rich, or maybe you'll end up with a bunch of useless code and a lesson in financial responsibility. Either way, it makes for great entertainment—especially when you're watching from the sidelines, shaking your head and enjoying the absurdity of it all.

Grumpy's Top Tips for Surviving the Cryptocurrency Craze

- **Don't Bet the Farm**

If you're going to invest, make sure it's money you don't mind losing. You wouldn't bet your retirement fund on a roulette wheel, so don't do it on Dogecoin either.

- **Password Management**

JWrite down your passwords. No, seriously, on paper. Somewhere safe. If you lose your key to your digital wallet, that's it. No do-overs.

- **Skip the NFTs**

Unless you genuinely enjoy looking at poorly drawn monkeys and have money to burn, skip the NFTs. Art is better when you can actually hang it on your wall.

- **Laugh from a Distance**

Crypto is a rollercoaster. If you're not up for the emotional ride, stay away. It's just as entertaining to watch other people go through the ups and downs without risking your own sanity.

In the end, cryptocurrency might be the most bizarre invention yet—a mix of high-tech promise, financial optimism, and plenty of confusion. Whether you dive in or watch from the sidelines, remember: if it feels like magic money, there's probably a trick involved. So sit back, enjoy the show—but don't lose your password.

Conclusion: "The Future is Here, and I'm Still Grumpy"

So, here we are. We've trudged through the mess of modern technology—grumbling about smartphones, muttering over social media, and laughing at the absurdities of digital assistants and cryptocurrency. If there's one thing I've learned, it's that no matter how "advanced" the world becomes, my grumpiness remains constant.

The future, with all its gadgets and miraculous code, promises convenience and connection. But often, it delivers a headache wrapped in Wi-Fi signals. And you know what? I'm okay with that. There's a strange joy in resisting technology's relentless march—believing we don't need an app for everything and that it's perfectly fine to mistrust a talking machine.

So, if you're like me—hanging on to some semblance of simplicity—take comfort. The future may be here, full of AI, invisible currencies, and gadgets that think they know best, but my determination to stay grumpy? That's here to stay too. Embrace the chaos, laugh at the absurdities, and remember: smart technology doesn't mean we can't be a little old-school. The world may change, but there's no update yet that will make me a fanboy. Stay grumpy, my friends.

Closing Thoughts: "Give Me a Break—and a Review!"

Well, there you have it—another grumpy, gripe-filled journey through the circus of modern technology. If you found yourself chuckling, nodding in agreement, or even just appreciating that someone else shares your irritation with all these digital headaches, then I'd say my work here is done. Now, if you're feeling particularly generous (or just want to help an old grump like me), I'd be incredibly grateful if you took a minute to leave a review. Your feedback doesn't just help other poor souls find this book—it's also proof that I'm not alone in my complaints.

If you didn't like it... well, that's your prerogative. But if you did, maybe it's time to spread the joy of grumpiness? Keep an eye out for upcoming titles like The Grumpy Old Man's Guide to Surviving Retirement and The Grumpy Old Man's Guide to Surviving Life with a Pet—because, let's face it, this world isn't getting any easier, and a little bit of shared exasperation goes a long way. Thanks for coming along for the ride. Stay grumpy, my friends!

The Grumpy Old Man's Guide to Surviving

MODERN TECHNOLOGY